The II-V-I Book

By David Bloom

Table of Contents

Fire and Form Series

Fire and Form symbolize the two basic materials in any art form. Fire represents personal expression. Form is the structural design in any artistic statement.

Great art is a statement of individuality. Creative freedom, not mere imitative slavery, requires the individual to find his/her voice. Creating one's personal statement is the ultimate artistic endeavor. However, one must first master the craft to make his unique statement. A serious artist must have both something to say and the means with which to say it.

Any musician who wills it can become a competent jazz player. The jazz artist must understand and be able to control the material, which will form the design for his/her personal statement of emotions. Jazz improvisation is the celebration of the moment through the spontaneous musical expression of the gamut of human emotions. However, it is not sufficient for a jazz musician to only express emotion without direction. In composition or improvisation, it is not enough just to create musical ideas; they must be developed and go somewhere.

This series is designed to show the artist how to go anywhere in a specific way. With this series we transcend the limitations of idiom and style, to give the artist creative freedom using the universe of musical possibilities available in Western harmony. The basic material for all Western music is the same (the chromatic scale). Style is the artist's choice.

The **Fire and Form Series** does not deal with the presentation of different styles. It deals with musical relationships and possibilities. The style and specific use of the material is the prerogative of the player.

In this series, hearing the material has equal importance with playing the music. All music is sound. It must be heard, either as an active listener or as an active creator. The active musical creator must be able to hear a sound, either from an outside source or in his/her head, and then be able to sing, write, or play that sound. Music that is played or written without being heard first is merely chance music, in which the player does not have control of his statement. Instead of the desired vivid articulate and expressive musical statement, the player is only producing sounds.

Each book in this series can be learned in three to four months, giving serious students a new vocabulary and direction in their quest for self-expression through music.

Introduction

The II-V-I chord progression represents the harmonic essence of Western harmony and is the most common chord progression in standard jazz tunes. The II-V-I Roman numerals are derived from the scale degrees that the chords are built on. In the C major scale (CDEFGABC) each note, or degree, has a chord built on it. The notes from the scale are stacked in thirds to form chords. C-E-G, a major triad, is the I chord because it is the chord that is built on the first note of the C major scale. D-F-A, which is D minor, is the II chord, because it is the chord built on the second note of the scale. These seven chords built from each note of the scale are called diatonic chords and can range from triads composed of 3 notes to 13th chords composed of 7 notes. The Roman numerals are used to indicate root movement or chord progressions. For example, I-VI-II-V in C major would be Cmaj7-Am7-Dm7-G7. The same is true of the C Harmonic minor scale. On each scale degree (CDEbFGAbB) a chord is built (Note: capital Roman numerals generally indicate a major chord while lower-case Roman numerals indicate minor chords - but for our purposes, we will capitalize all of them for consistency).

The serious player must be able to negotiate this chord progression in order to improvise well. One has to learn to hear and be fluent with all 24 major and minor scales. Mastery of these materials will prepare the serious musician to improvise on countless tunes. Jazz musicians use many possible scales to "fit" or "color" these chord changes. The initial scales included here are representative of the harmony favored by jazz improvisers in the 1960's, but there are numerous alternatives included in the back of this book for you to try. To begin improvising we will use only two scales: the major scale and the harmonic minor scale.

Diatonic 7th Chords Built from the Scale Degrees in C Major

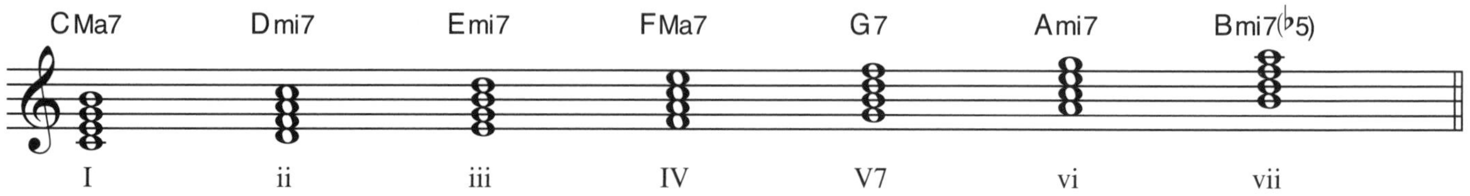

Diatonic 7th Chords Built from the Scale Degrees in C Harmonic Minor

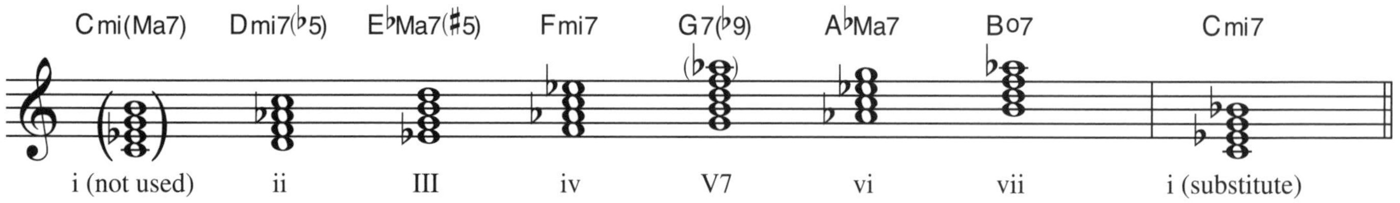

For major II-V-I we will use the major scale of the intended tonic. For example, the first II-V-I in the book, Dm7-G7-Cmaj7, is in C major. Hence we will use the C major scale to improvise on all three chords as their tones are generated from the C major scale.

In the preceding examples the C major scale, the C harmonic minor scale and the diatonic seventh chords generated by the respective scales are shown. Every note (degree) of the scale has a chord built on it. These four note chords - called diatonic 7th chords - are built by stacking the scale in thirds (C-E-G-B, D-F-A-C etc. in the major scale, and C-Eb-G-B, D-F-Ab-C etc. in the harmonic minor scale). The preceding sequence is the same for all major and harmonic minor scales. For minor II-V-I's we will use the harmonic minor scale on the II and the V but when we resolve to the I chord we will use the dorian mode. For example, in C minor for Dm7b5 and G7b9 we will use C harmonic minor because those two chords are derived from the C harmonic minor scale. When we resolve to the I we will substitute Cm7 for CmMaj7 and use the C dorian mode. Very often minor II-V-I's will resolve to a minor 7th chord instead of the minor major 7th and as a result will not use a harmonic or melodic minor scale but will use the dorian mode on the minor 7th chord. If the minor II-V resolves to a I minor major 7th chord, then the melodic minor scale is used. Remember, the scale you use is determined by the chord quality.

You will notice in both the major and minor II-V-I exercises that each scale or mode used starts on the root of the chord. In the Major II-V-I (Dm7 - G7 - C), on Dm7 we play the C major scale starting on "D". On G7, we play the C major scale starting on "G", and on the Cmaj7 we play the C major scale starting on "C". In the Minor II-V-I (Dm7b5 - G7b9 - Cm7), on Dm7b5 we play the C harmonic minor scale starting on D. On G7b9 we play the C harmonic minor starting on G, and on Cm7 we play Bb major starting on C.

Practice Procedure

I. You must know exactly what you're going to do BEFORE you start each exercise.

II. Practice sessions must be goal oriented.

III. Cleanliness in execution must be imperative.

IV. Gaining authority should be the goal of practice.

V. Strict rhythm must always be maintained:

a) Strict realization of rhythmic values
b) Strict tempo maintenance

VI. Use the entire dynamic range.

VII. Never practice longer than concentration can be maintained. To practice sloppily is not effective practice. It also shows a disrespect for one's abilities and potential.

VIII. Practice with a tape recorder to evaluate what you have achieved in each practice session. Listen back to the tape to hear how precise you were in your practicing. Did you achieve the QUALITY OF EXECUTION you were looking for?

IX. You must learn to ENJOY YOUR PRACTICING. Take pride in the intensification and focus of your being. If it is a chore, proper relaxation and musicality will not happen.

X. If you make or accept mistakes in execution you are NOT practicing effectively.

Step by Step

1. Play the first scale and broken chord (arpeggios) exercise with a metronome marking (MM) at 60=quarter note
2. After you can play them perfectly ten times, sing them at MM 60=quarter note.
3. Play the exercise for track 2 of the **II-V-I** background recording. Play through the first exercise ten times, making sure that you play all the right notes in perfect time. It would be a good idea to record yourself frequently in order to monitor your improvement. It is essential that you develop very focused practicing habits in the beginning. There should be no errors. If there are any, then back up and play the scales and chords slow enough so that they are played perfectly. Only after you can play them consistently perfect you have earned the skill to play faster.
4. Improvise on track 2 using the broken chords and scales. Use as many ways to break up the scales as you can. Also use as many different rhythms and rest values as you can. The object is to develop as much variety of phrasing as you can. Record and assess yourself for rhythmic variety, rest value variety, accuracy of notes, resolution of ideas and overall expression and message.
5. Repeat steps 1-4 for all the other exercises. After you can play on tracks 2-13 with mastery of the materials, try using any of the alternative scales scales or colors to use on the **II-V-I's**. You can use any of the scales in each column with any of the scales in the other columns. Just make sure to use the scales on the chord indicated on top of the column.

Practice Time Allocation

For the most effective results, this book should be used in one of the following ways. Your time availability and commitment will determine which of the following methods will best work for you.

Play through Tracks 2-13 each and every day. (approx. 35-45 min.)

Play through two Major and Minor **II-V-I** Tracks each and every day. In this way you will have played through all twelve keys and all the Turn-Arounds in just three days. (approx. 20-30 min.)

Play through 1 Major and Minor **II-V-I** Track and one or two Turn-Around Tracks each and every day. Using this practice regimen, you will have played through all twelve keys and all the Turn-Arounds in just 6 days. (approx. 10-20 min.)

Play through 1 Major and Minor **II-V-I** Track and one or two Turn-Around Tracks per week for 6 weeks. You can repeat the same tracks every day or use any combination of the aforementioned practice regimens.

Special Note

All twelve major and minor keys are represented in the following six tracks (i.e. Tracks 2-7). Each track consists of two 16-bar sections with repeats. Each 16-bar strain consists of a major key **II-V-I** progression and a corresponding minor key **II-V-I** progression. Therefore, each track takes you through a total of four keys. The groove of each track changes from "Swing" to a "Bossa Nova" beat on the second time through the entire exercise.

Exercises for Major and minor II-V-Is in all Keys

Exercises for track No. 2

Track continues on following page.

Exercises for track No. 2 (Continued)

Fine
Track completed.

Exercises for track No. 3

Track continues on following page.

Exercises for track No. 3 (Continued).

Track completed.

Exercises for track No. 4

Track continues on following page.

Exercises for track No. 4 (Continued).

Track completed.

Exercises for track No. 5

Track continues on following page.

Exercises for track No. 5 (Continued).

Track completed.

Exercises for track No. 6

Track continues on following page.

Exercises for track No. 6 (Continued).

Fine

Track completed.

Exercises for track No. 7

Track continues on following page.

Exercises for track No. 7 (Continued).

Fine

Track completed.

Exercises for Major and minor II-V-Is in all Keys

Exercises for track No. 2

Track continues on following page.

Exercises for track No. 2 (Continued).

Track completed.

Exercises for track No. 3

Track continues on following page.

Exercises for track No. 3 (Continued).

Track completed.

Exercises for track No. 4

Track continues on following page.

Exercises for track No. 4 (Continued).

Track completed.

Exercises for track No. 5

Track continues on following page.

Exercises for track No. 5 (Continued).

Track completed.

Exercises for track No. 6

Track continues on following page.

Exercises for track No. 6 (Continued).

Track completed.

Exercises for track No. 7

Track continues on following page.

Exercises for track No. 7 (Continued).

Fine

Track completed.

Exercises for Major and minor II-V-Is in all Keys

Exercises for track No. 2

Track continues on following page.

Exercises for track No. 2 (Continued).

Fine

Track completed.

Exercises for track No. 3

Track continues on following page.

Exercises for track No. 3 (Continued).

Track completed.

Exercises for track No. 4

Track continues on following page.

Exercises for track No. 4 (Continued).

Fine

Track completed.

Exercises for track No. 5

Track continues on following page.

Exercises for track No. 5 (Continued).

Fine

Track completed.

Exercises for track No. 6

Track continues on following page.

Exercises for track No. 7 (Continued).

Track completed.

Exercises for track No. 7

Track continues on following page.

Exercises for track No. 7 (Continued).

Track completed.

Major and Minor II-V-I in all keys

Track No. 2

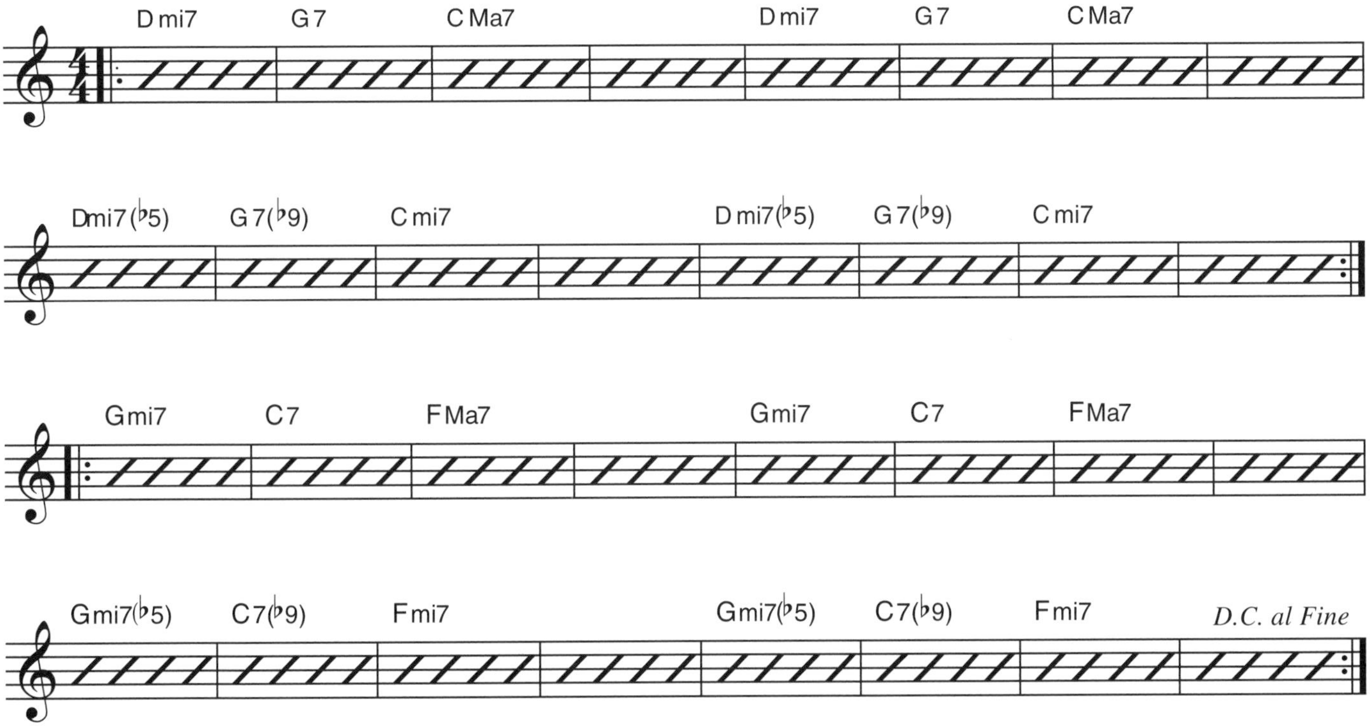

Track No. 3

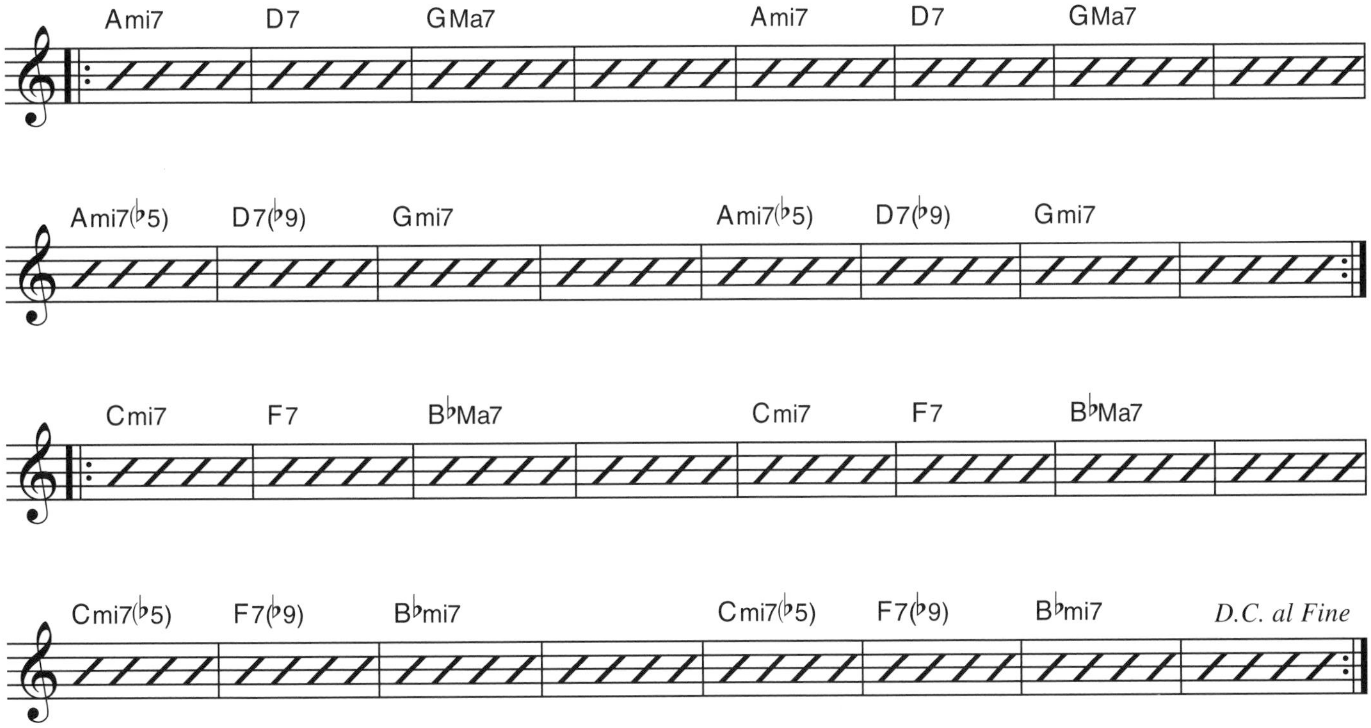

C Instruments

Track No. 4

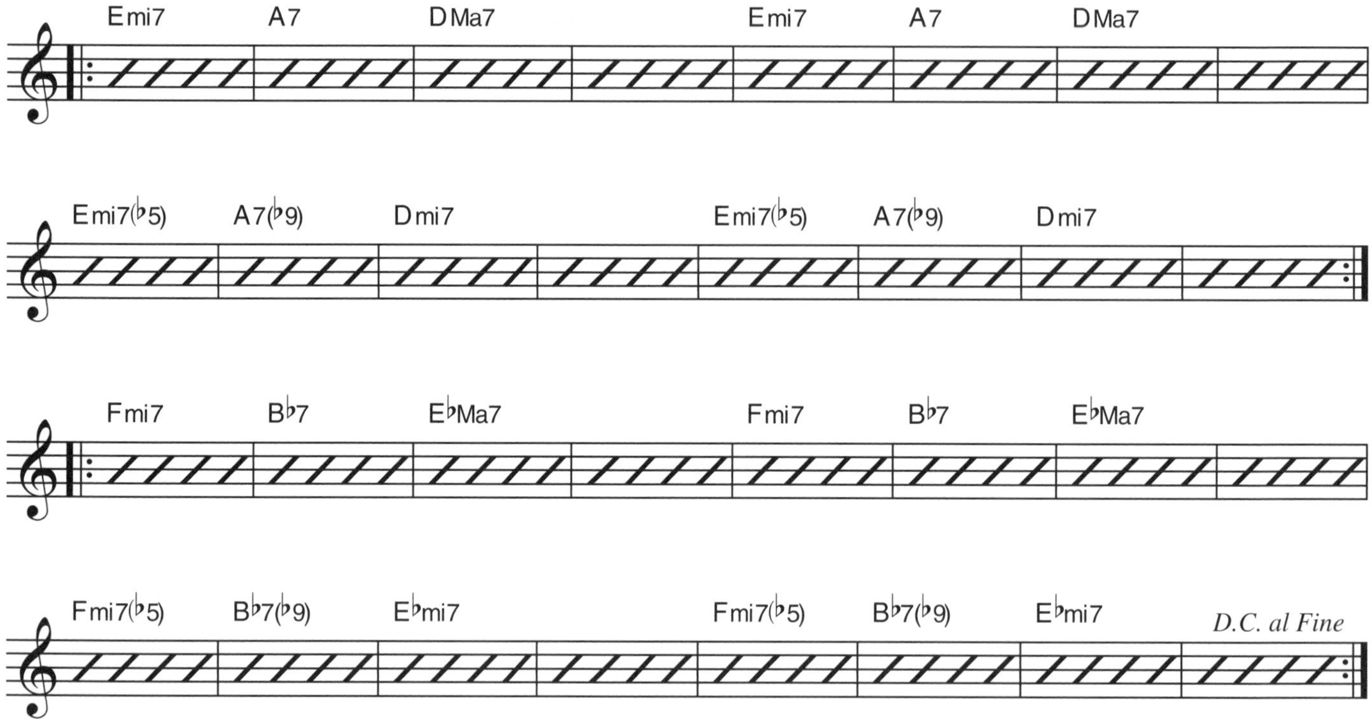

Track No. 5

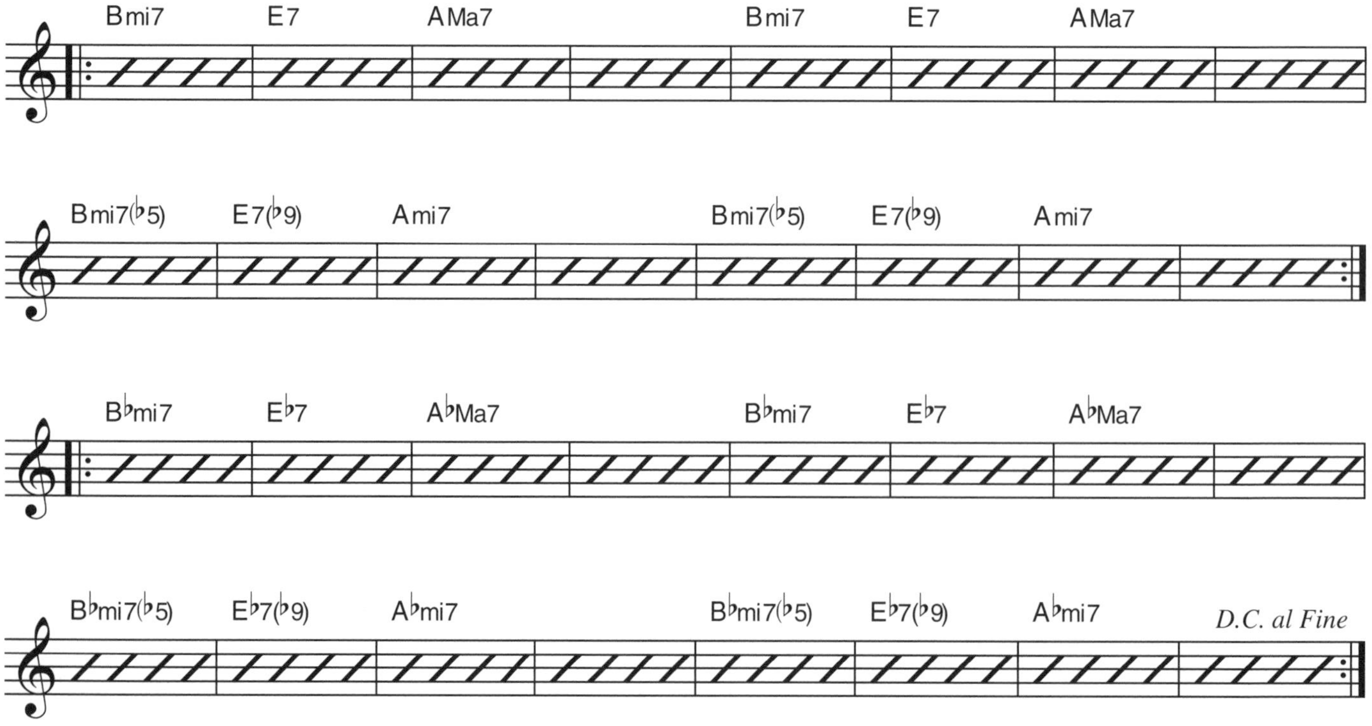

Emi7 A7 DMa7 Emi7 A7 DMa7
Emi7(♭5) A7(♭9) Dmi7 Emi7(♭5) A7(♭9) Dmi7
Fmi7 B♭7 E♭Ma7 Fmi7 B♭7 E♭Ma7
Fmi7(♭5) B♭7(♭9) E♭mi7 Fmi7(♭5) B♭7(♭9) E♭mi7
D.C. al Fine
Bmi7 E7 AMa7 Bmi7 E7 AMa7
Bmi7(♭5) E7(♭9) Ami7 Bmi7(♭5) E7(♭9) Ami7
B♭mi7 E♭7 A♭Ma7 B♭mi7 E♭7 A♭Ma7
B♭mi7(♭5) E♭7(♭9) A♭mi7 B♭mi7(♭5) E♭7(♭9) A♭mi7
D.C. al Fine

Track No. 6
F♯mi7 B7 EMa7 F♯mi7 B7 EMa7
F♯mi7(♭5) B7(♭9) Emi7 F♯mi7(♭5) B7(♭9) Emi7
E♭mi7 A♭7 D♭Ma7 E♭mi7 A♭7 D♭Ma7
E♭mi7(♭5) A♭7(♭9) D♭mi7 E♭mi7(♭5) A♭7(♭9) D♭mi7
D.C. al Fine
Track No. 7
A♭mi7 D♭7 G♭Ma7 A♭mi7 D♭7 G♭Ma7
A♭mi7(♭5) D♭7(♭9) G♭mi7 A♭mi7(♭5) D♭7(♭9) G♭mi7
C♯mi7 F♯7 BMa7 C♯mi7 F♯7 BMa7
C♯mi7(♭5) F♯7(♭9) Bmi7 C♯mi7(♭5) F♯7(♭9) Bmi7
D.C. al Fine

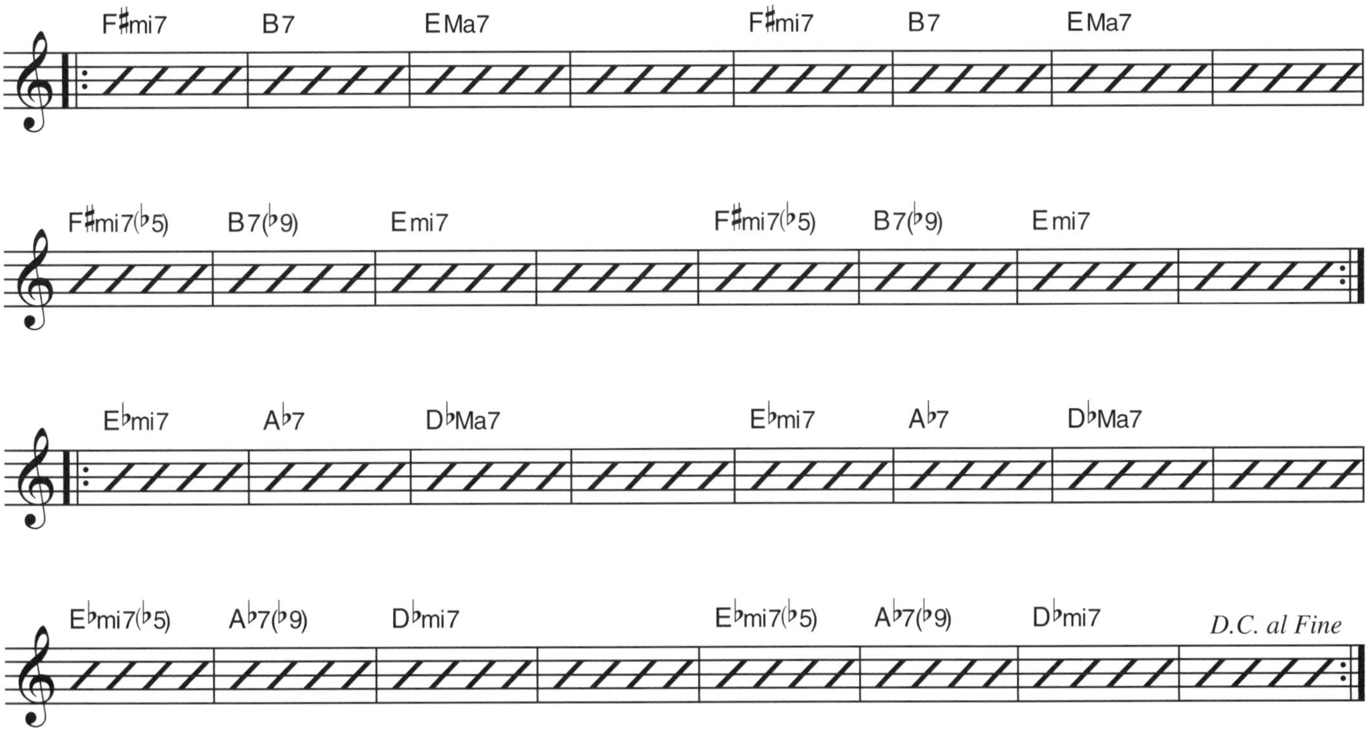

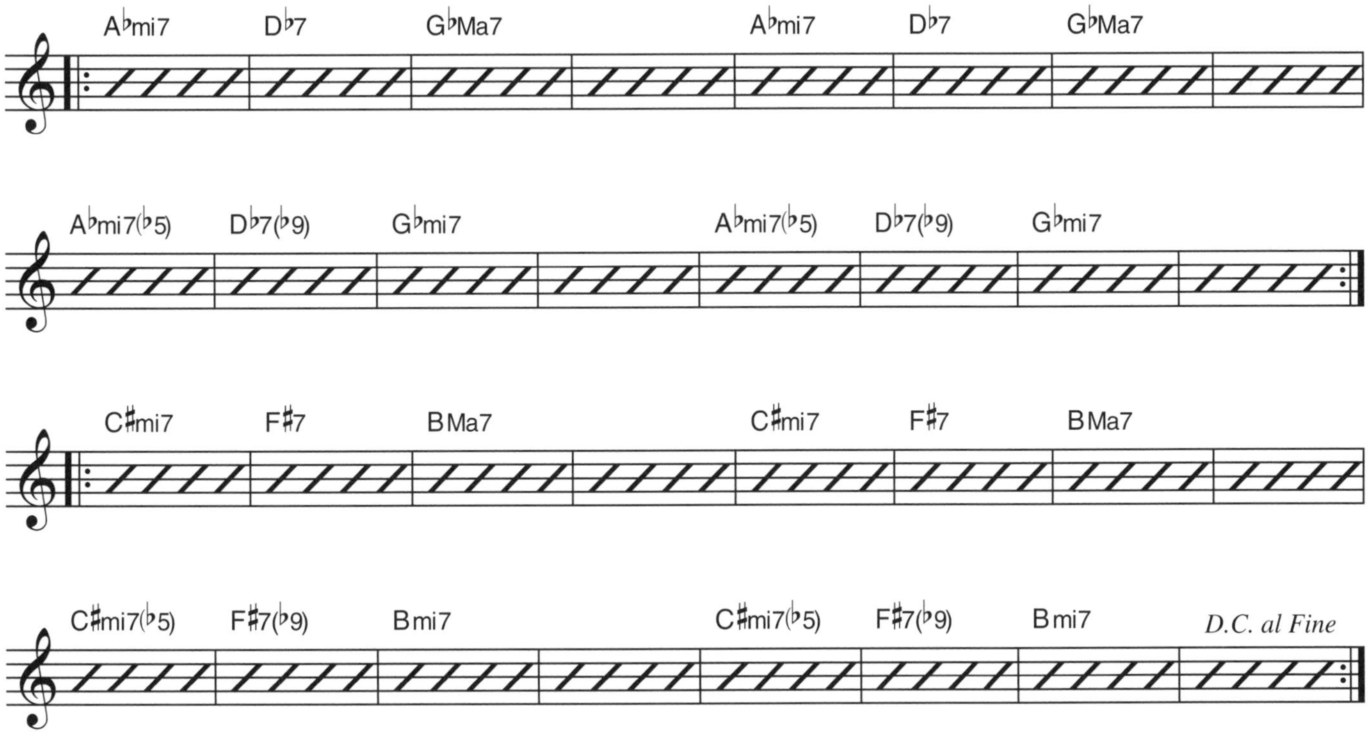

Turn-Arounds

Track No. 8

Play eight times with a swing feel; then play eight times with a bossa nova feel.

Track No. 9

Play eight times with a swing feel; then play eight times with a bossa nova feel.

Track No. 10

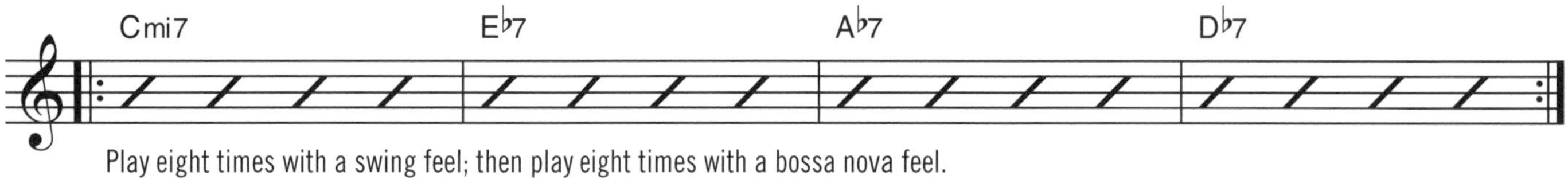

Play eight times with a swing feel; then play eight times with a bossa nova feel.

Track No. 11

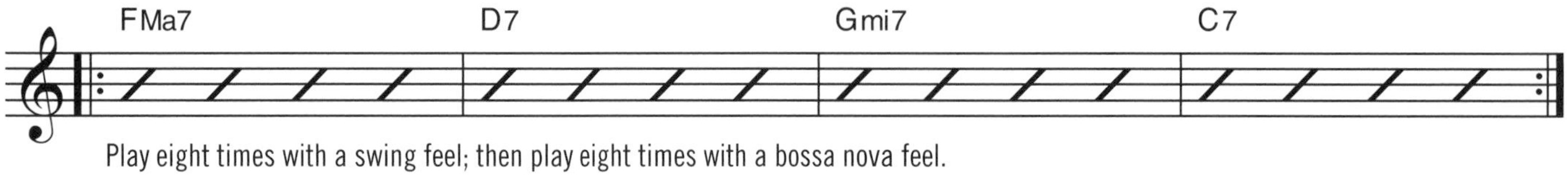

Play eight times with a swing feel; then play eight times with a bossa nova feel.

Track No. 12

Play eight times with a swing feel; then play eight times with a bossa nova feel.

Track No. 13

Play eight times with a swing feel; then play eight times with a bossa nova feel.

Track No. 14

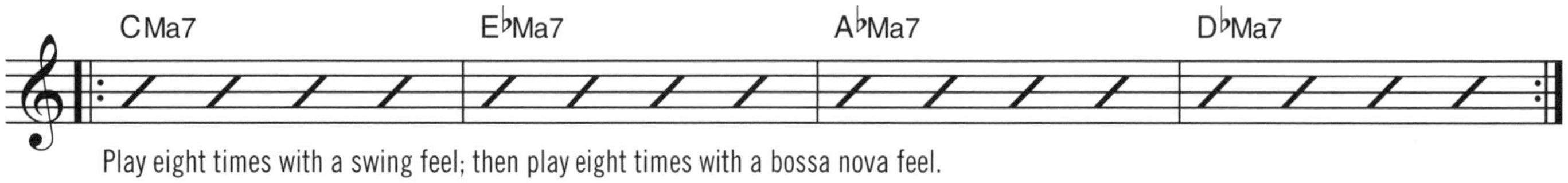

Play eight times with a swing feel; then play eight times with a bossa nova feel.

Major and Minor II-V-I in all keys

Track No. 2

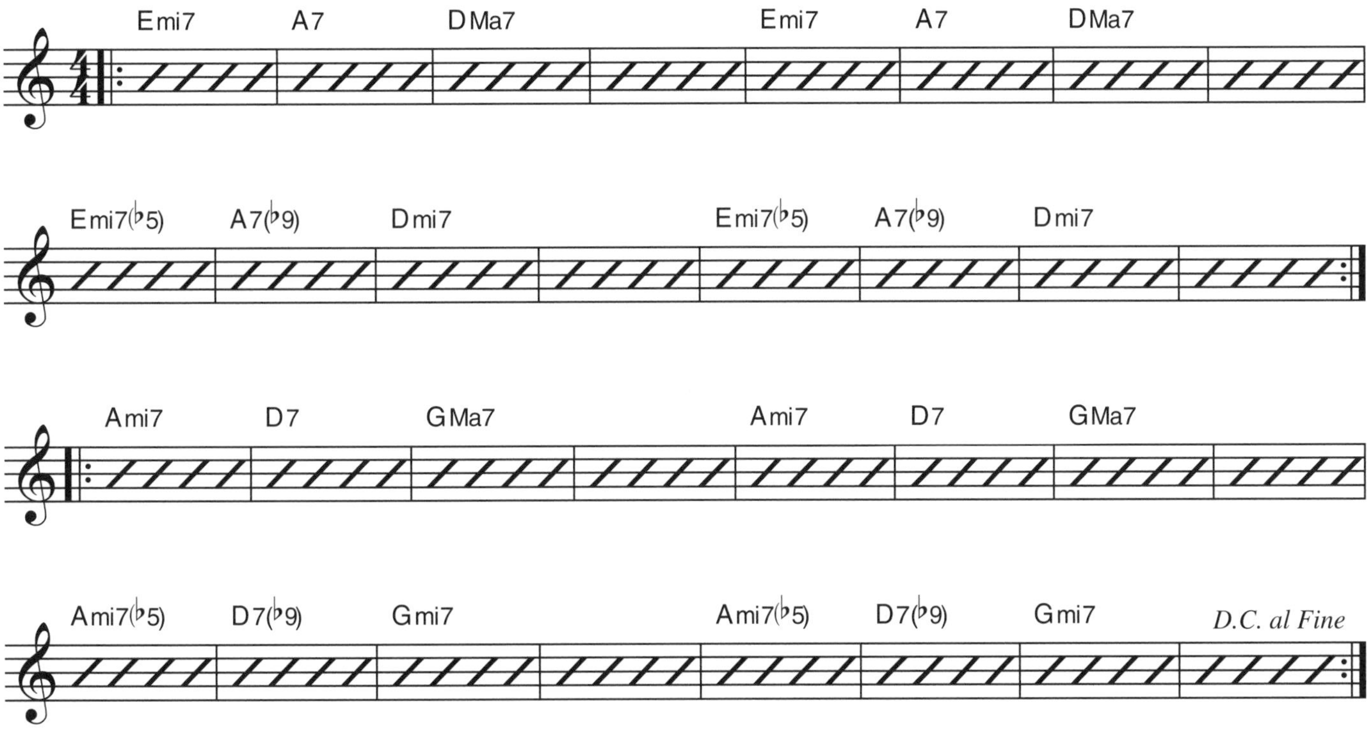

Track No. 3

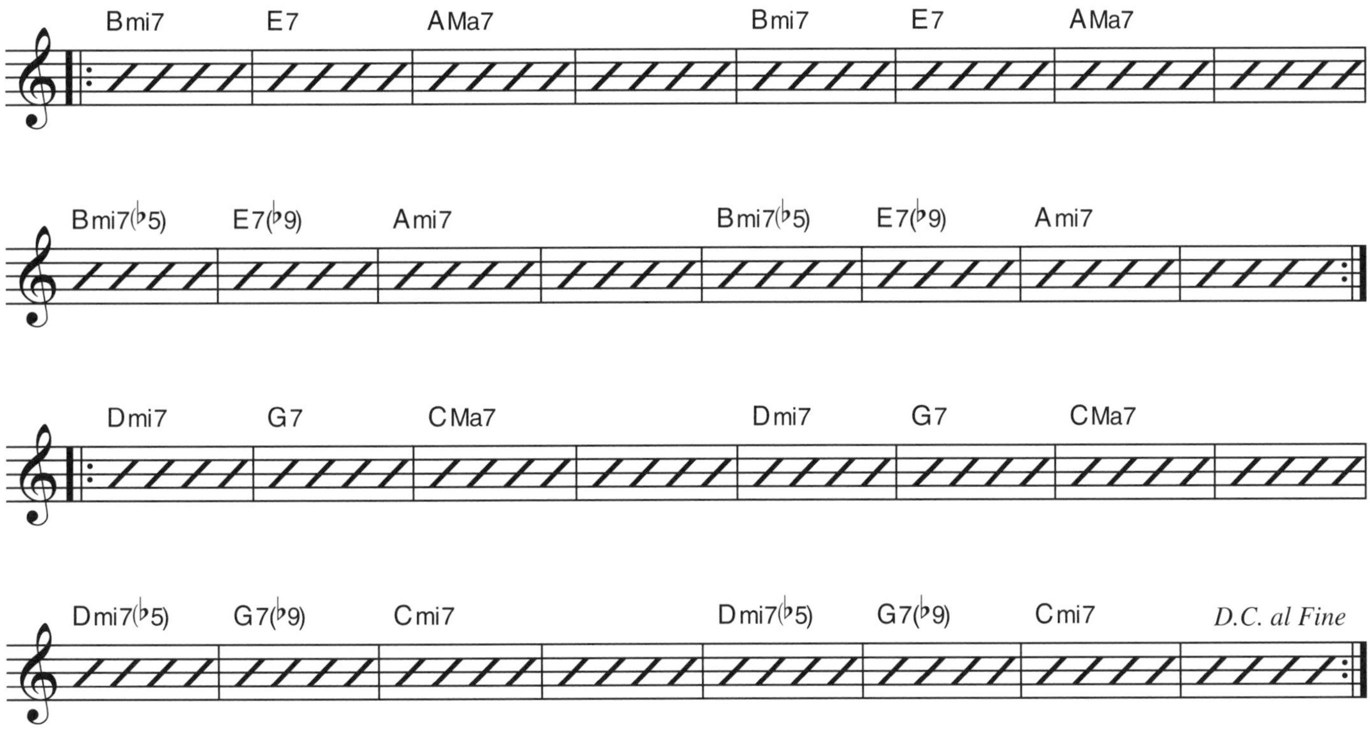

Track No. 4

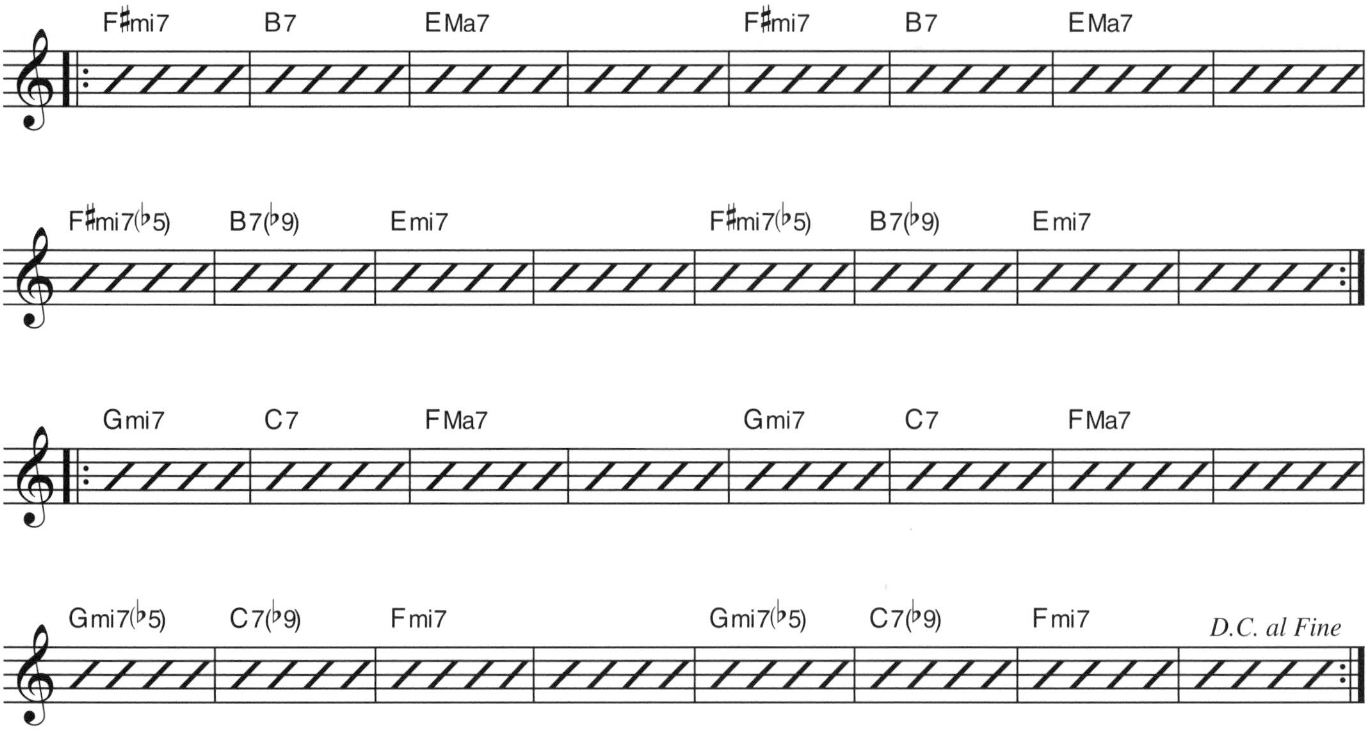
F♯mi7 B7 EMa7 F♯mi7 B7 EMa7
F♯mi7(♭5) B7(♭9) Emi7 F♯mi7(♭5) B7(♭9) Emi7
Gmi7 C7 FMa7 Gmi7 C7 FMa7
Gmi7(♭5) C7(♭9) Fmi7 Gmi7(♭5) C7(♭9) Fmi7
D.C. al Fine

Track No. 5

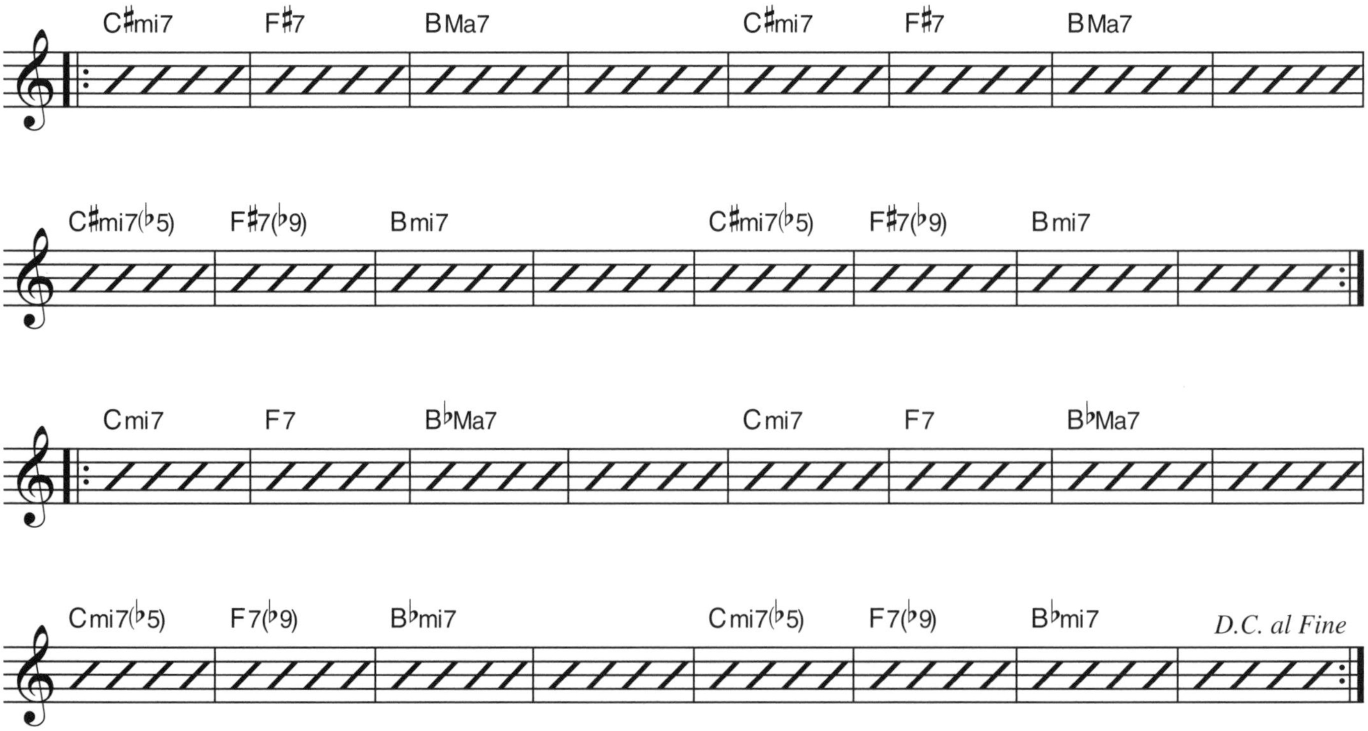
C♯mi7 F♯7 BMa7 C♯mi7 F♯7 BMa7
C♯mi7(♭5) F♯7(♭9) Bmi7 C♯mi7(♭5) F♯7(♭9) Bmi7
Cmi7 F7 B♭Ma7 Cmi7 F7 B♭Ma7
Cmi7(♭5) F7(♭9) B♭mi7 Cmi7(♭5) F7(♭9) B♭mi7
D.C. al Fine

Track No. 6

A♭mi7 D♭7 G♭Ma7 A♭mi7 D♭7 G♭Ma7
A♭mi7(♭5) D♭7(♭9) G♭mi7 A♭mi7(♭5) D♭7(♭9) G♭mi7
Fmi7 B♭7 E♭Ma7 Fmi7 B♭7 E♭Ma7
Fmi7(♭5) B♭7(♭9) E♭mi7 Fmi7(♭5) B♭7(♭9) E♭mi7
D.C. al Fine
Track No. 7
B♭mi7 E♭7 A♭Ma7 B♭mi7 E♭7 A♭Ma7
B♭mi7(♭5) E♭7(♭9) A♭mi7 B♭mi7(♭5) E♭7(♭9) A♭mi7
E♭mi7 A♭7 D♭Ma7 E♭mi7 A♭7 D♭Ma7
E♭mi7(♭5) A♭7(♭9) D♭mi7 E♭mi7(♭5) A♭7(♭9) D♭mi7
D.C. al Fine

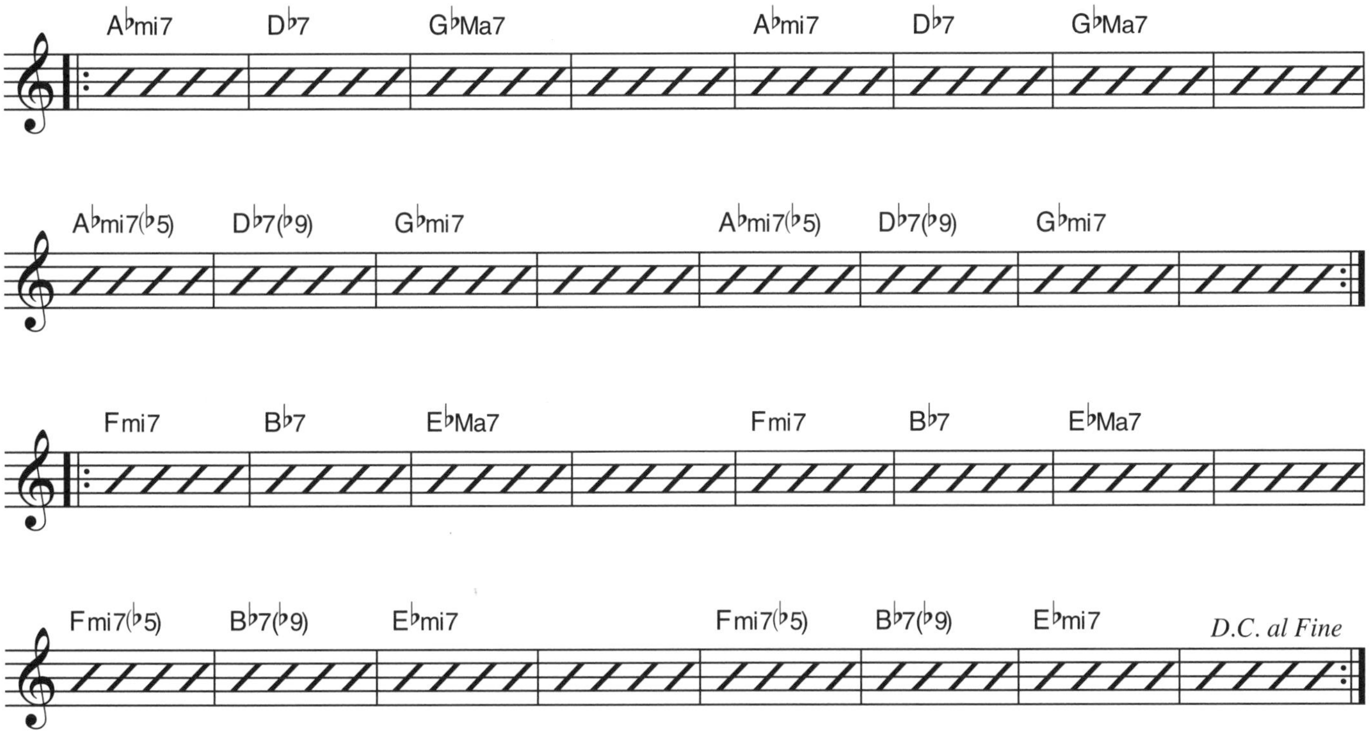

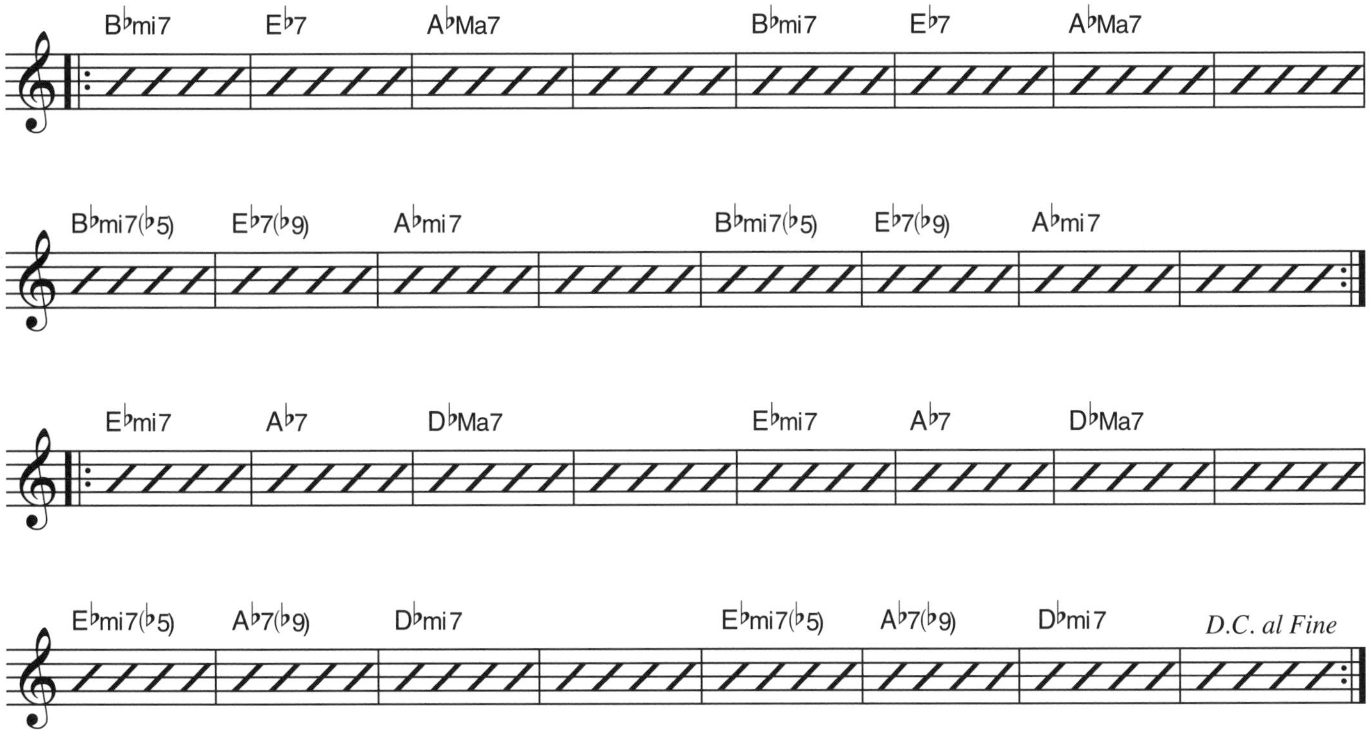

Turn-Arounds

Track No. 8

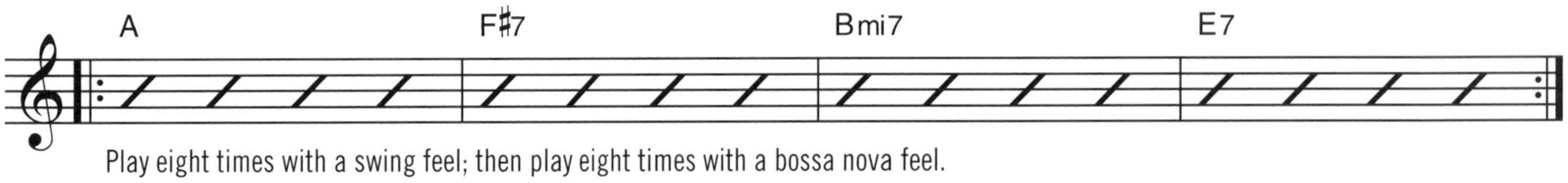

Play eight times with a swing feel; then play eight times with a bossa nova feel.

Track No. 9

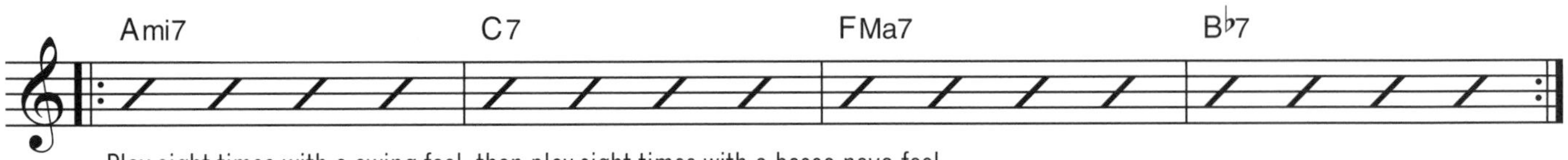

Play eight times with a swing feel; then play eight times with a bossa nova feel.

Track No. 10

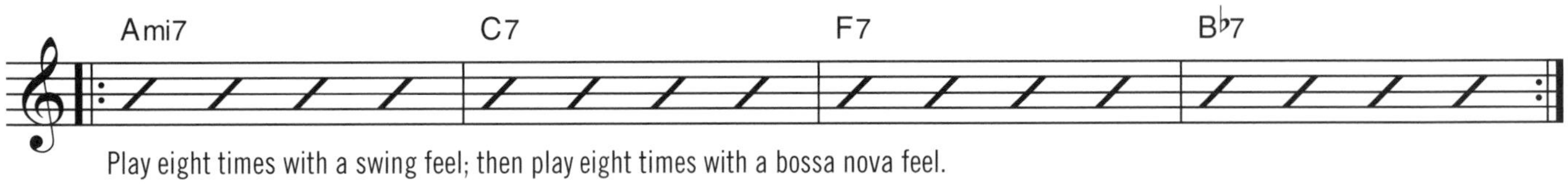

Play eight times with a swing feel; then play eight times with a bossa nova feel.

Track No. 11

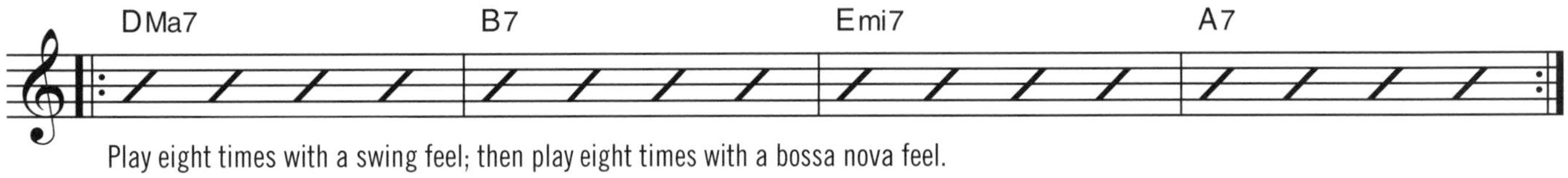

Play eight times with a swing feel; then play eight times with a bossa nova feel.

Track No. 12

Play eight times with a swing feel; then play eight times with a bossa nova feel.

Track No. 13

Play eight times with a swing feel; then play eight times with a bossa nova feel.

Track No. 14

Play eight times with a swing feel; then play eight times with a bossa nova feel.

Major and Minor II-V-I in all keys

Track No. 2

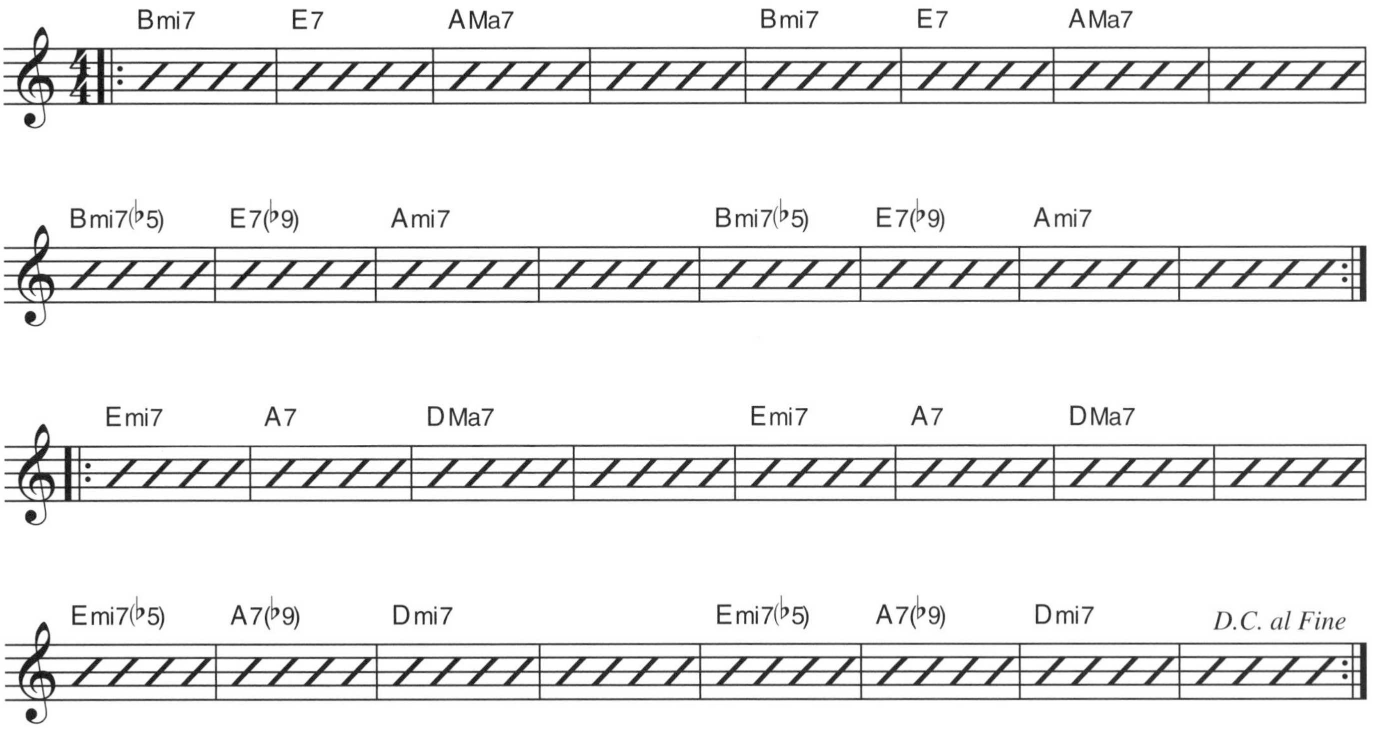

Track No. 3

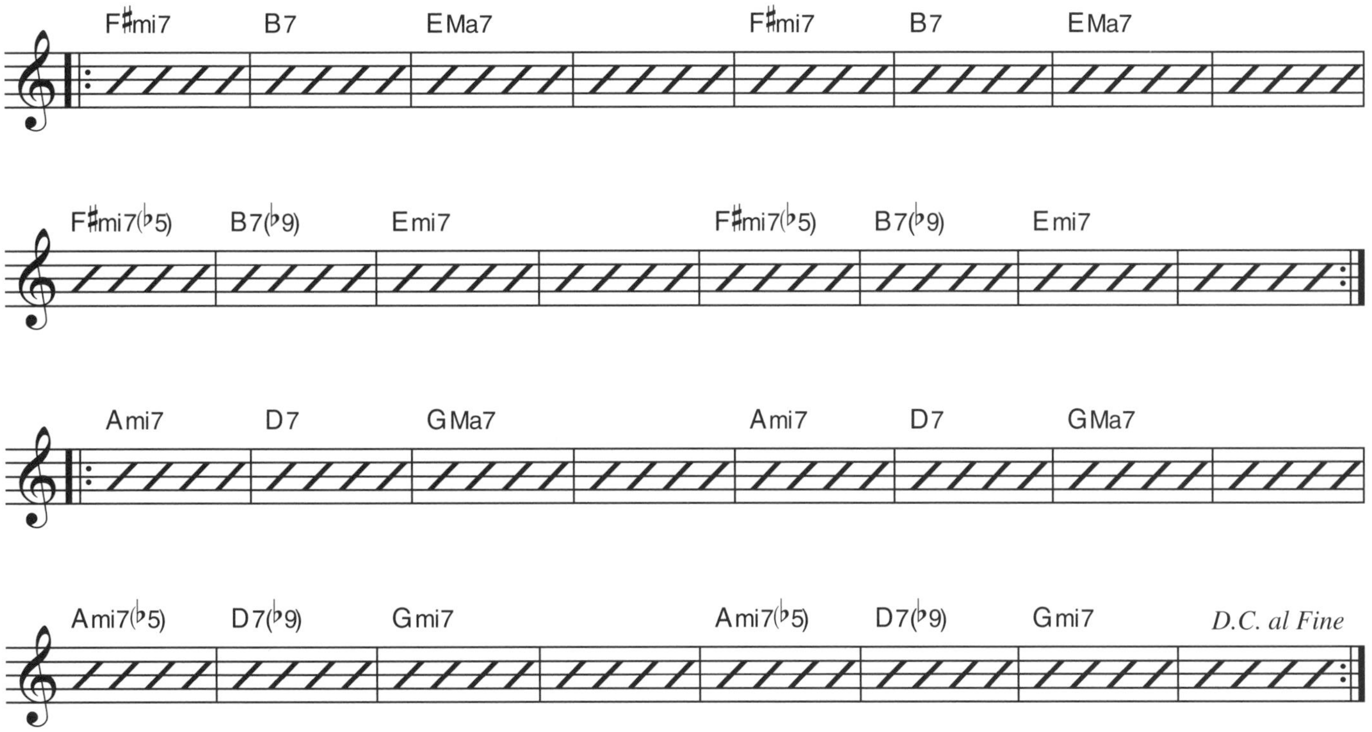

Track No. 4

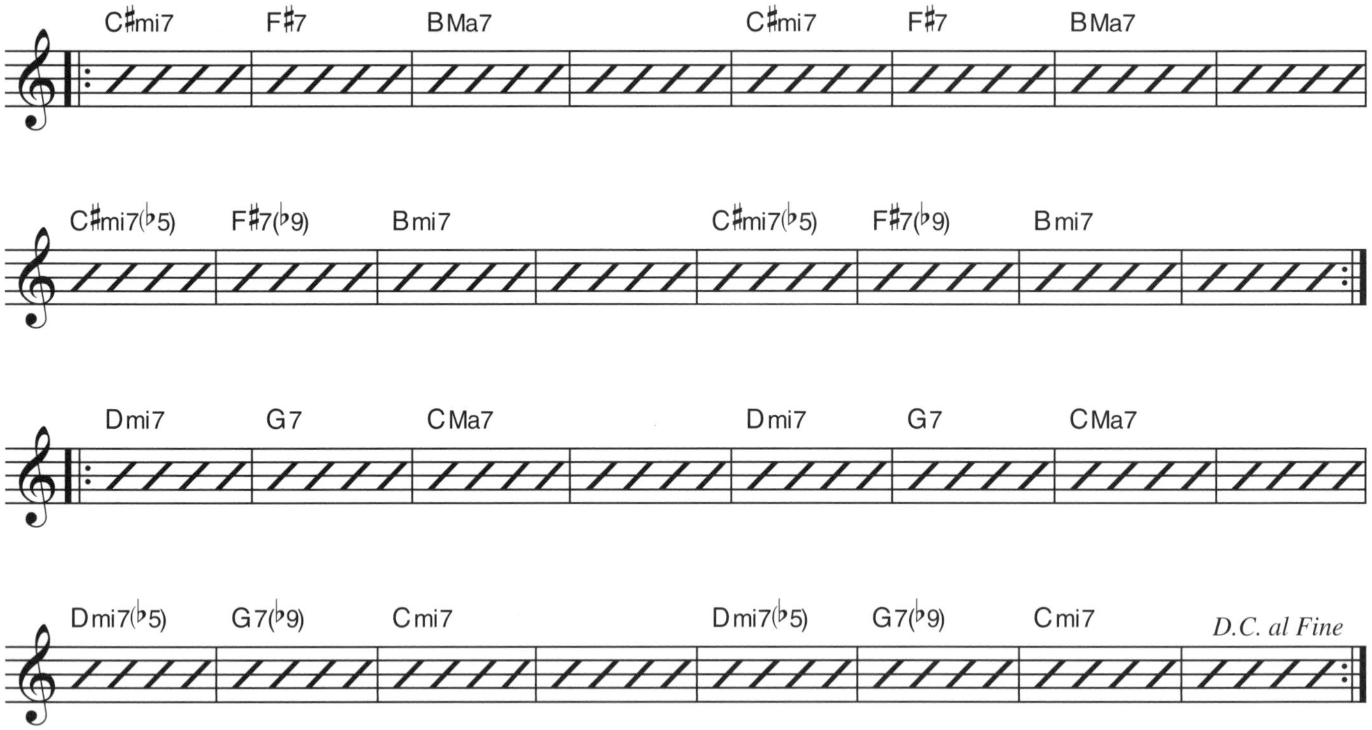

Track No. 5

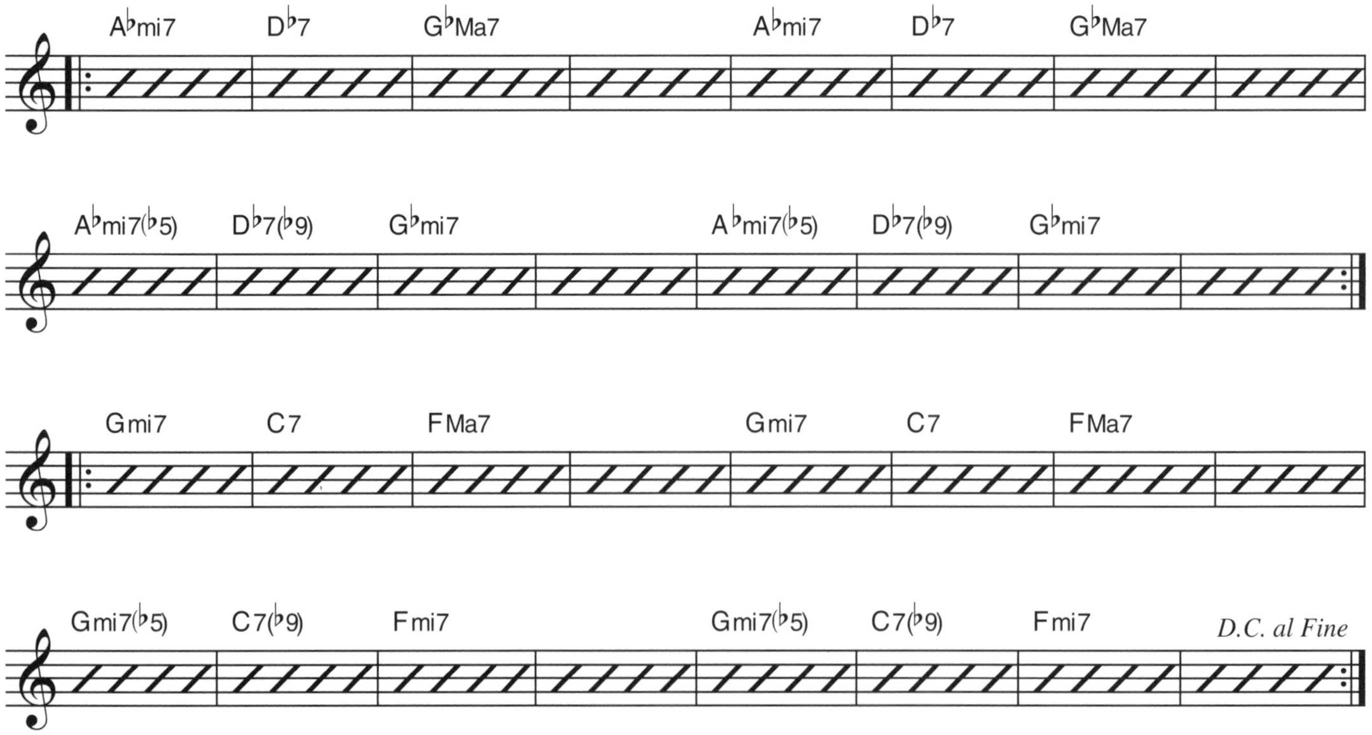

Track No. 6
E♭mi7
A♭7
D♭Ma7
E♭mi7
A♭7
D♭Ma7
E♭mi7(♭5)
A♭7(♭9)
D♭mi7
E♭mi7(♭5)
A♭7(♭9)
D♭mi7
C mi7
F7
B♭Ma7
C mi7
F7
B♭Ma7
C mi7(♭5)
F7(♭9)
B♭mi7
C mi7(♭5)
F7(♭9)
B♭mi7
D.C. al Fine
Track No. 7
F mi7
B♭7
E♭Ma7
F mi7
B♭7
E♭Ma7
F mi7(♭5)
B♭7(♭9)
E♭mi7
F mi7(♭5)
B♭7(♭9)
E♭mi7
B♭mi7
E♭7
A♭Ma7
B♭mi7
E♭7
A♭Ma7
B♭mi7
E♭7
A♭Ma7
B♭mi7
E♭7
A♭Ma7
D.C. al Fine

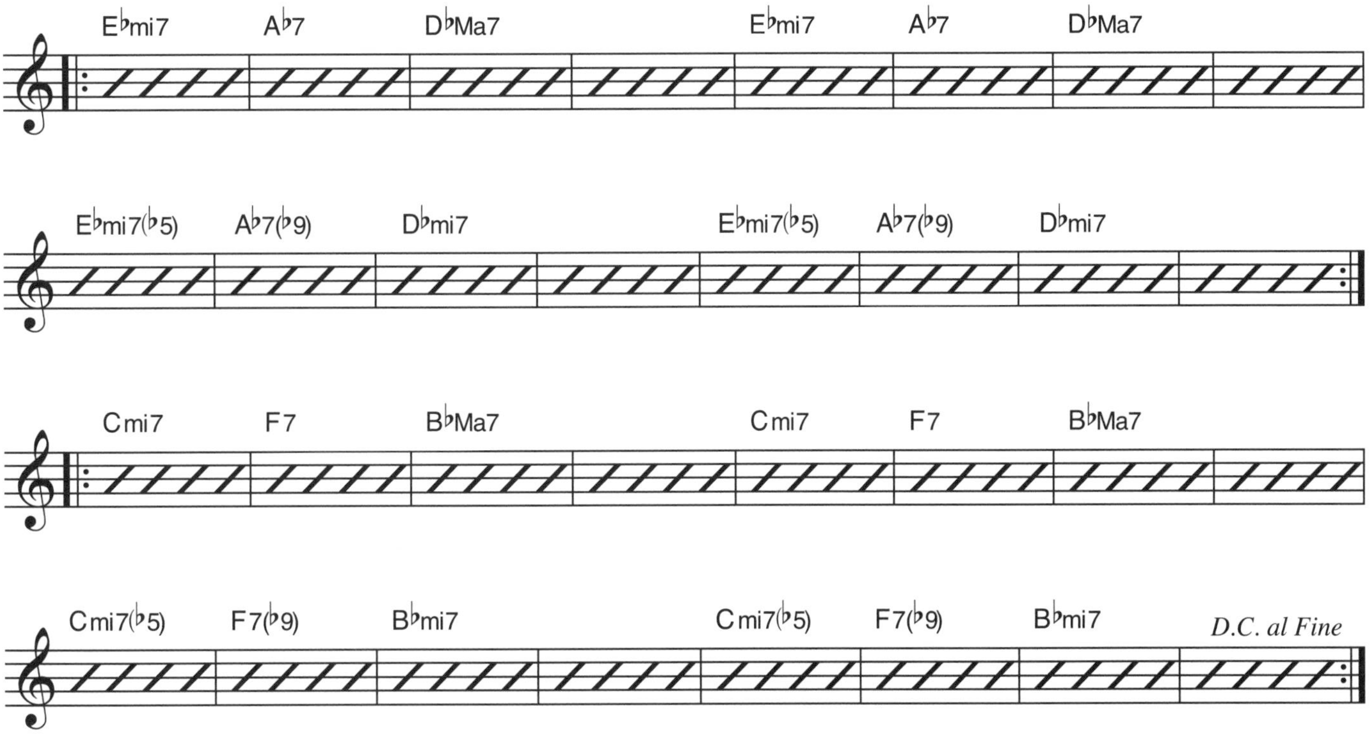

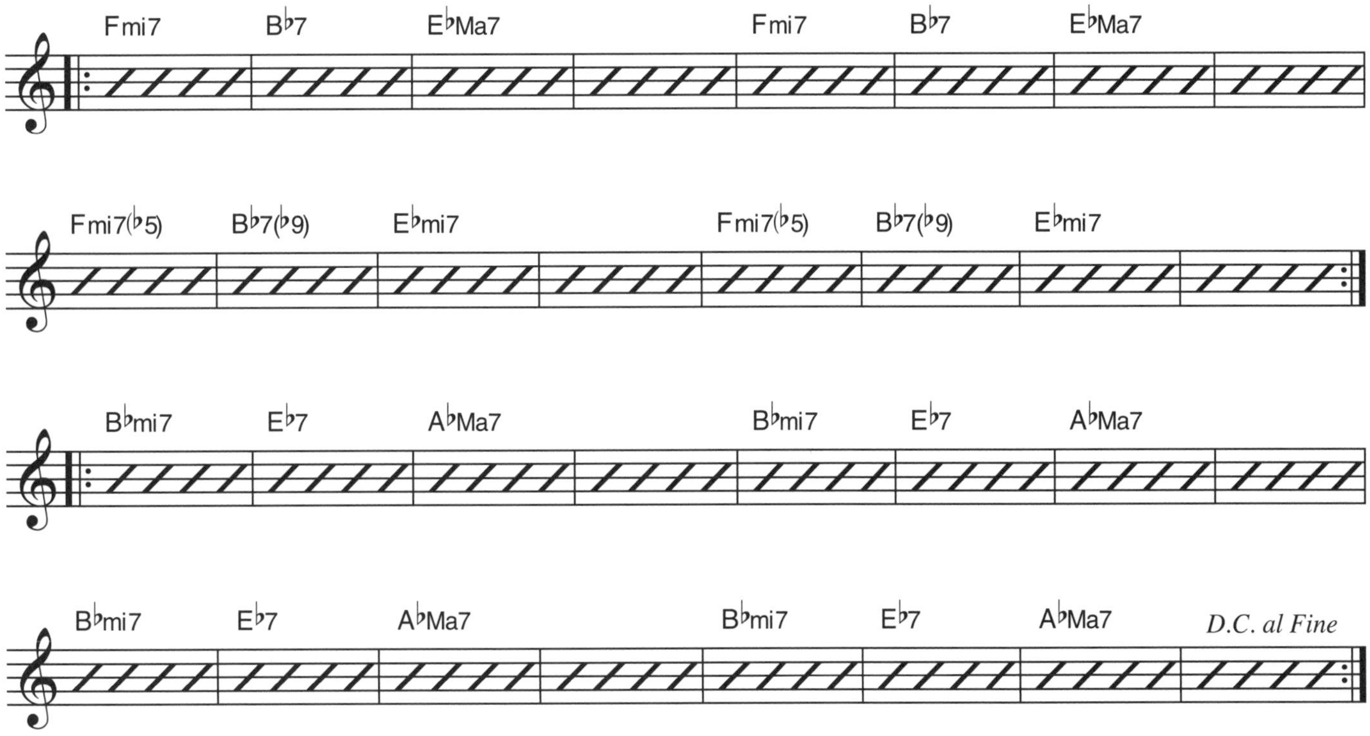

Turn-Arounds

Track No. 8

Play eight times with a swing feel; then play eight times with a bossa nova feel.

Track No. 9

Play eight times with a swing feel; then play eight times with a bossa nova feel.

Track No. 10

Play eight times with a swing feel; then play eight times with a bossa nova feel.

Track No. 11

Play eight times with a swing feel; then play eight times with a bossa nova feel.

Track No. 12

Play eight times with a swing feel; then play eight times with a bossa nova feel.

Track No. 13

Play eight times with a swing feel; then play eight times with a bossa nova feel.

Track No. 14

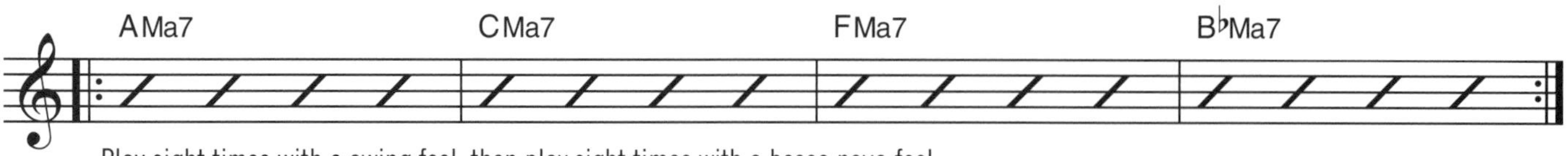

Play eight times with a swing feel; then play eight times with a bossa nova feel.

Scale Materials for Major II-V-I's

C Major

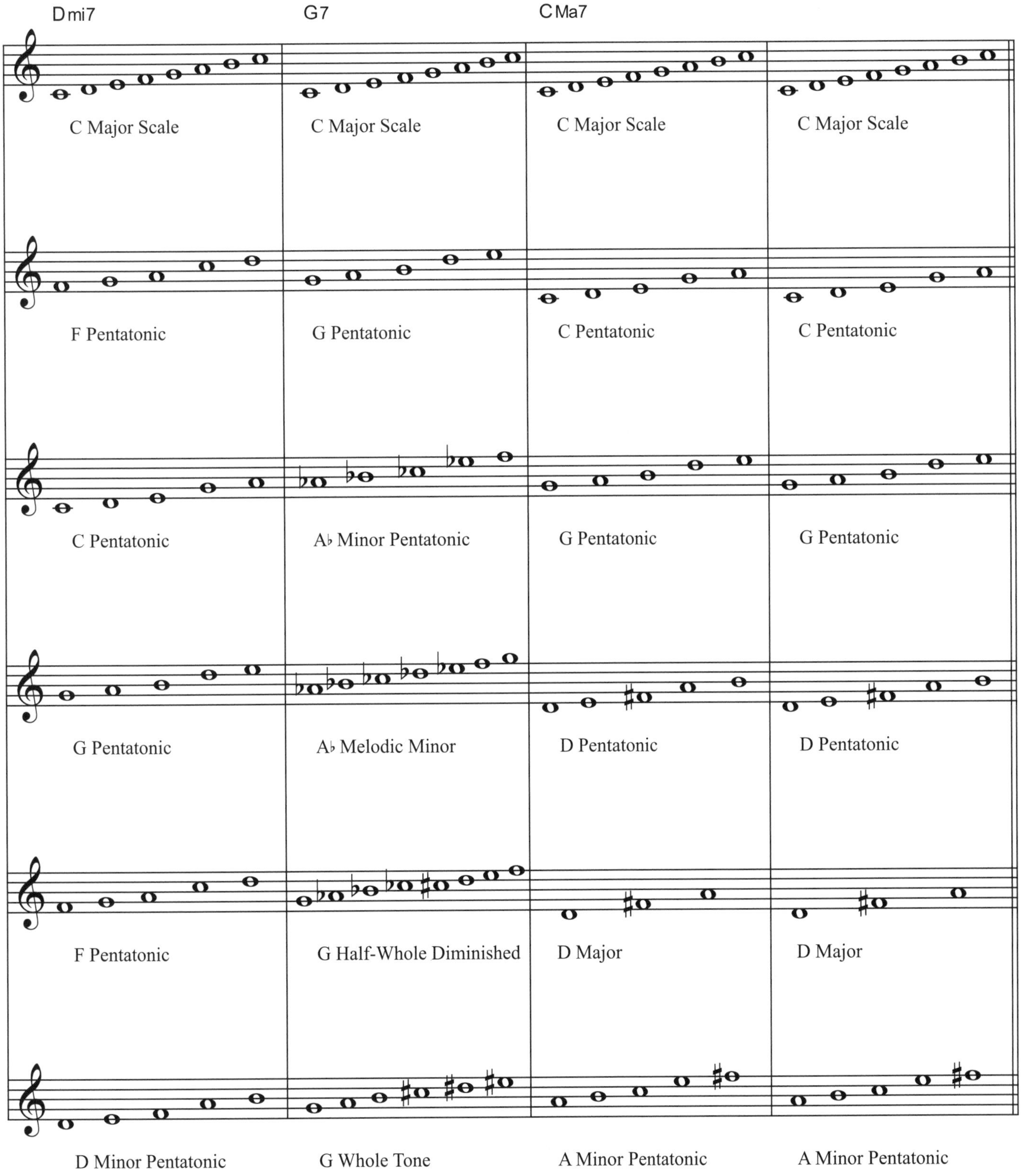

Scale Materials for Minor II-V-I's

C Minor

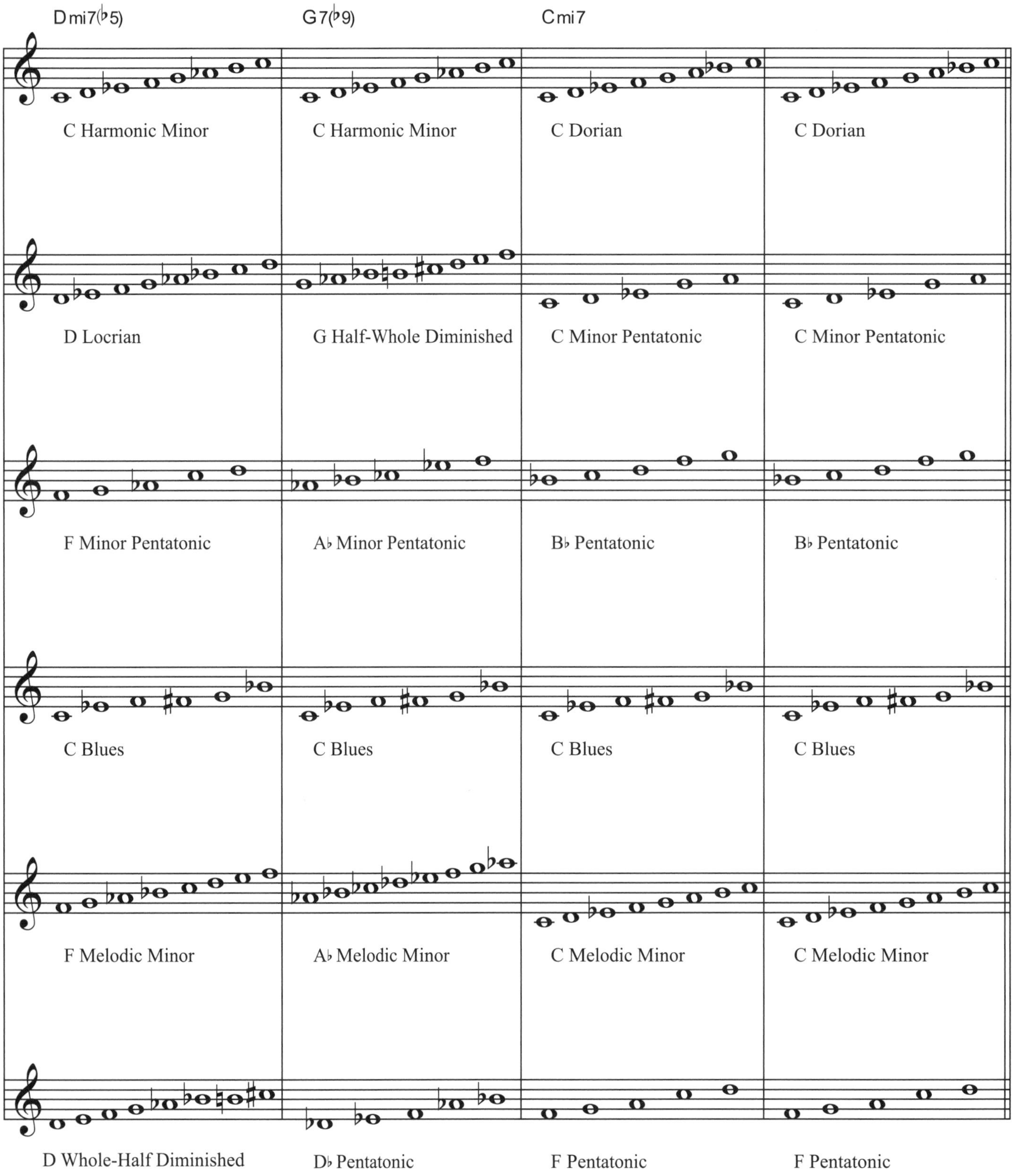

Major II V I
Scale Mixtures

Major II V I
Scale Mixtures

Minor II V I
Scale Mixtures

Minor II V I
Scale Mixtures

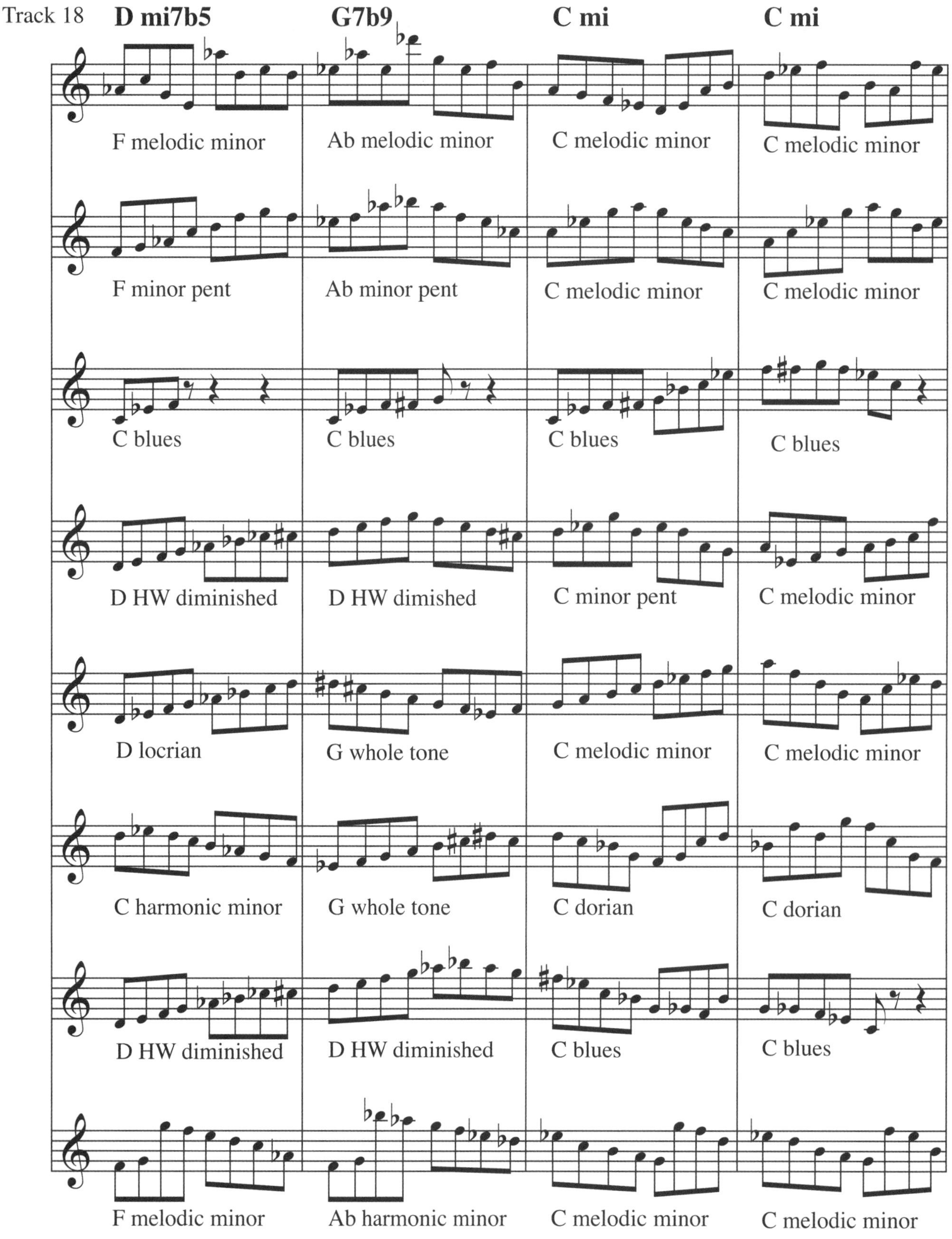

II V I
Polychords

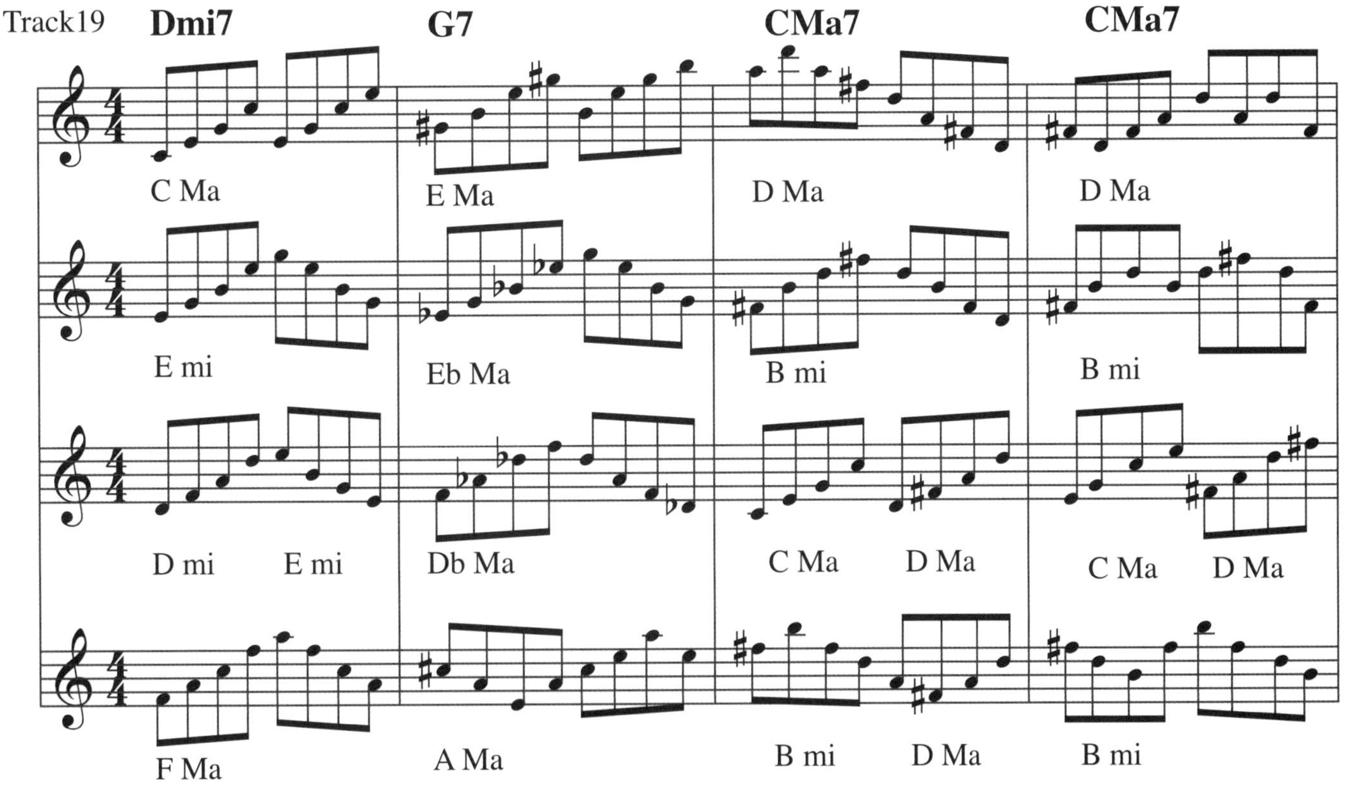

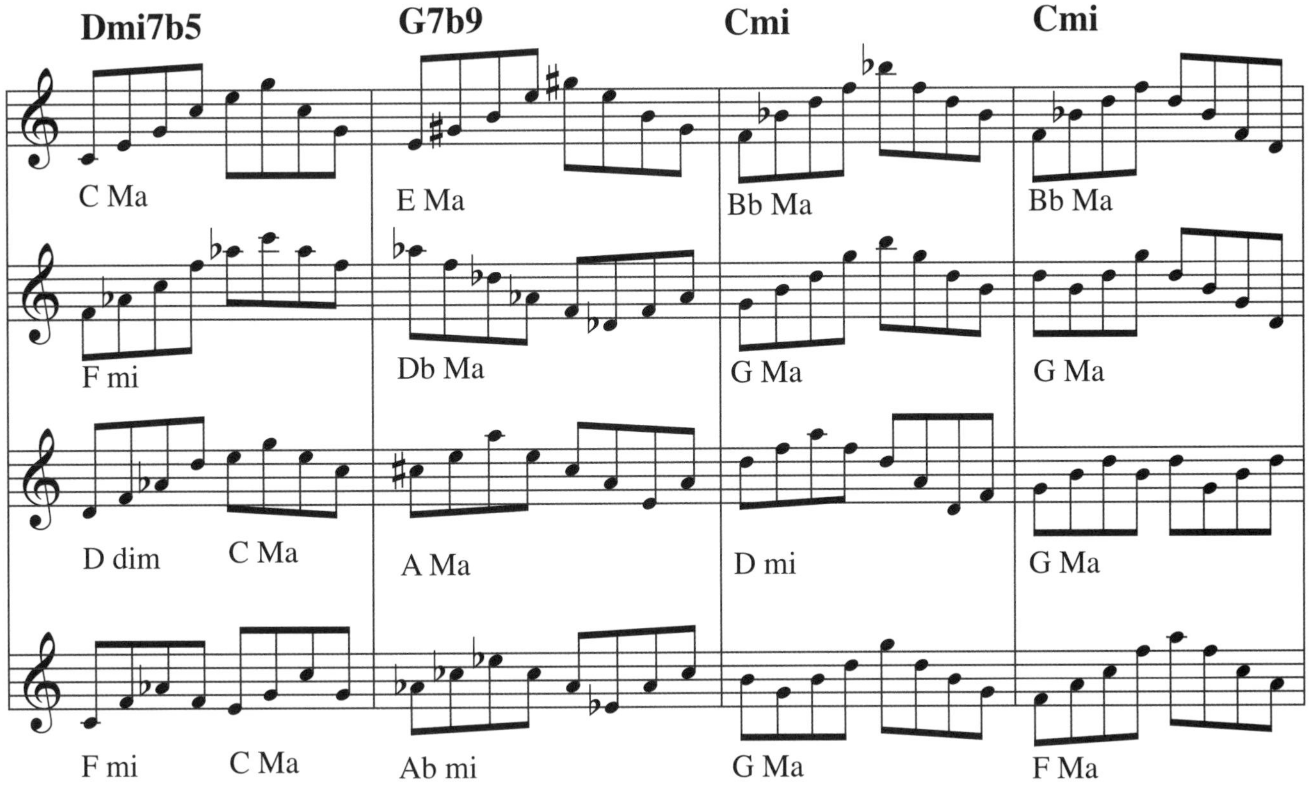

II V I

Write your own phrases using the scales indicated

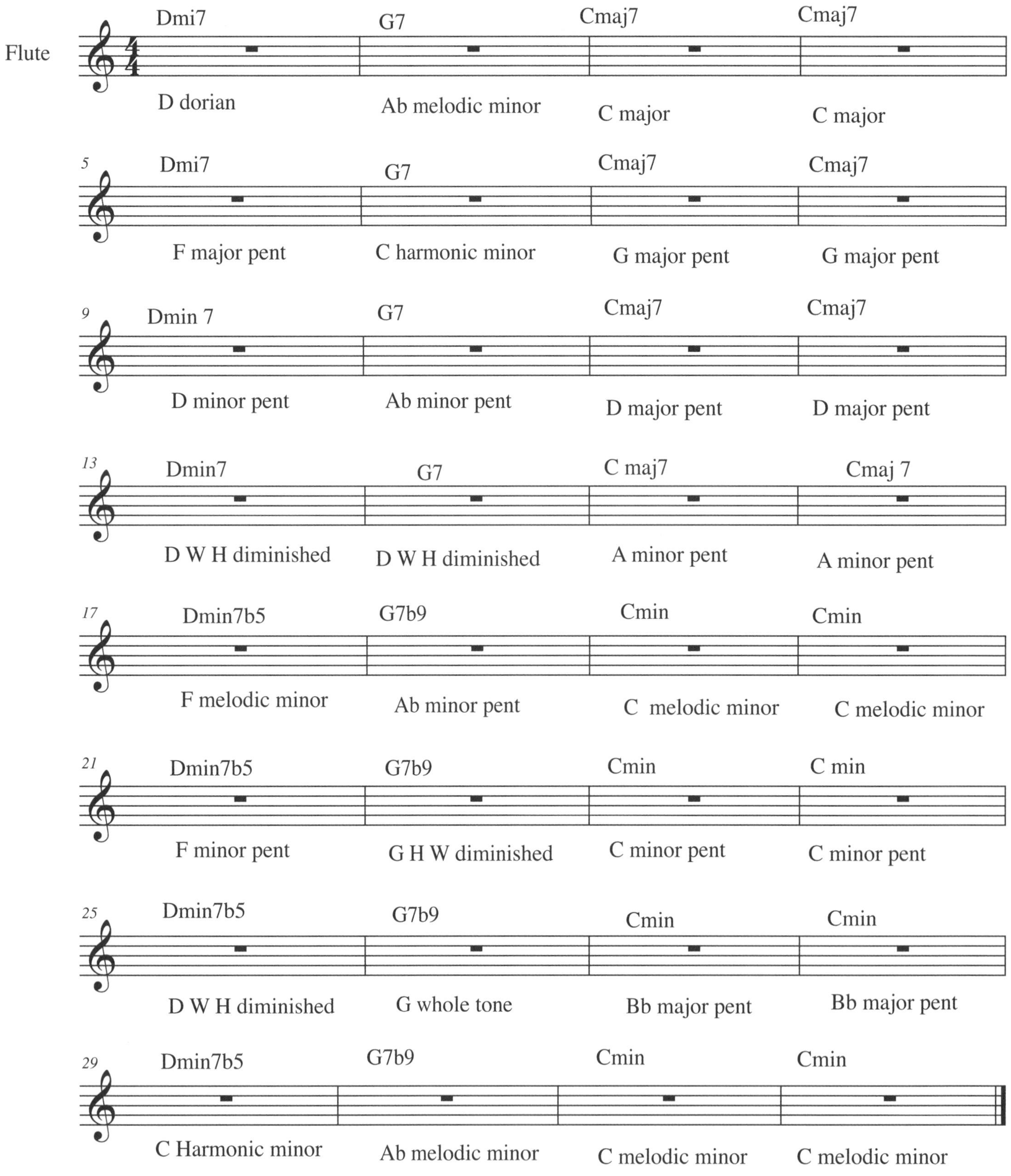

CRACK THE CODE

WITH BOOK/CD SETS FROM

BLOOM SCHOOL OF JAZZ PUBLISHING

MAJOR BLUES FOR GUITAR VOL. 1
HL00695979
Become fluent with colorful major blues chord progressions in three months. Make the blues sound fresh at your gig tonight. Contains 21 melodic major blues chord progressions.
CD included. $19.95

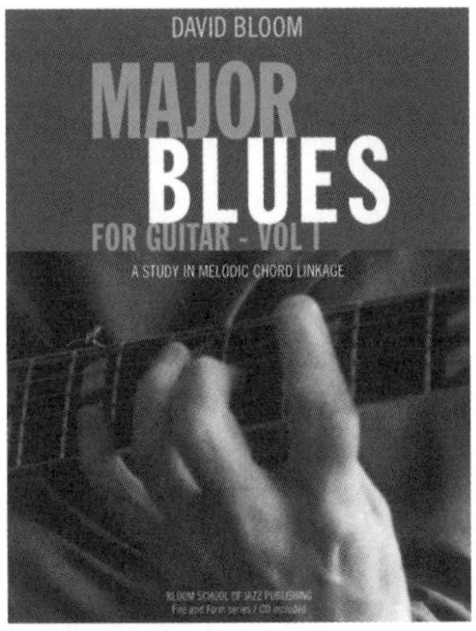

"I just received and enjoyed your two books with CD's Major Blues Vol.1 and Minor Blues Vol.1. These are both great books for anyone who really wants to swing with the blues. Nice layout with cool fingerings. The playing on the CD's is great and very inspiring; I was jamming along in no time. Thanks."

JOE SATRIANI
Guitar legend

MINOR BLUES FOR GUITAR VOL. 1
HL00695980
Discover highly melodic minor blues chord progressions and become fluent with them in three months. Gives you the freedom to play minor blues differently every time. Contains 21 melodic minor blues chord progressions.
CD included. $19.95

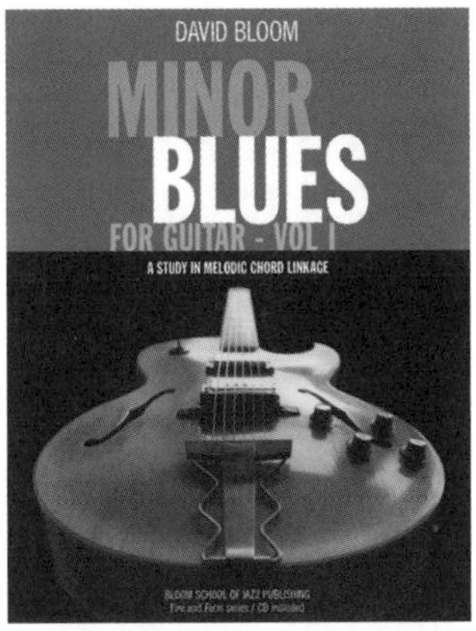

"David's 30 years of concentrated teaching experiences have now yielded a series of well-thought-out publications so all of us can gain from his insights. Now, David's unique methods and philosophies are available to musicians everywhere."

DON SICKLER
Five-time Grammy winning producer
Second Floor Music

MELODIC CHORDS FOR GUITAR VOL. 1
HL00695981
Tremendously increase your melodic chord vocabulary for soloing, chord-melodies and comping. This unique book arranges chords not only by chord type (major 7th, minor 7b5, etc.) but also by all available chord tones (1, 3, 5, 7, 9, 11, 13). Learn chords that express your emotions.
CD included. $19.95

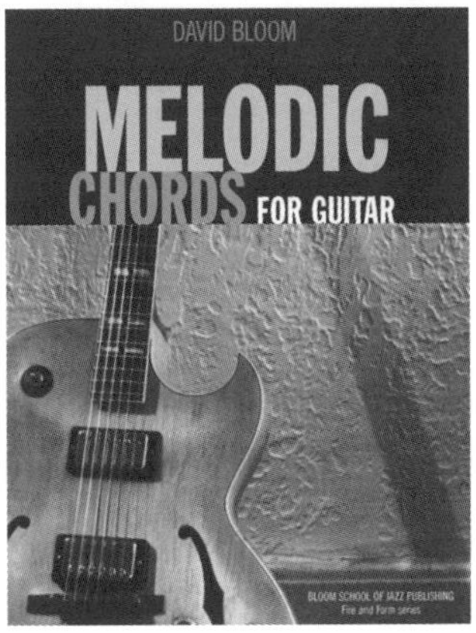

"David Bloom is a wonderful player, composer and teacher. The books that he's written are invaluable. Clearly written and very thorough. I highly recommend David Bloom's books to players of all levels."

MIKE STERN
Guitar Legend

EXCLUSIVELY DISTRIBUTED BY
HAL•LEONARD®

www.bloomschoolofjazz.com • Phone: 312-957-9300 •
Bloom School of Jazz, 218 South Wabash, Suite 600 Chicago, IL 60604

BLOOM SCHOOL OF JAZZ
218 S. Wabash, #600
Chicago, IL 60604
Phone: 312-957-9300
Fax: 312-957-0133
email: dbloom1@interaccess.com
www.bloomschoolofjazz.com